PRAISE FOR BETSY L. JORDAN

"Being Betsy's client changed my outlook on life. There are self-help books, motivational movies, thoughtful quotes that give you a 'hmmm' moment, but there's nothing like the direct dynamic impact of Betsy's approach. There is such a thing as a mental shift, or altering your mind-set. I know this now, because Betsy Jordan helped me accomplish quite a shift with her unique coaching methods. Thank you Betsy for making all the difference in my world, I have a much better grasp on business and financial responsibility than ever before."

—Daniel Jones

"Betsy, brings a great energy and enthusiasm to her work. Creative, concise and fun to work with."

—Joseph C. D'Alessandro
Independent Media Production Professional

"I hired Betsy for executive coaching, and it was one of the best decisions I've made in a while. She revitalized key aspects of my career with her thoughtful and disciplined methodology. She is so intelligent and empathetic, yet she'll tell you when your full of sh*t when you need to hear it. I highly recommend her to turbo-charge your life."

—Chip Venters

CEO at BrowsePlay Interactive Video

"Betsy is an inspired leader with energy and passion to share her many gifts and talents. I recommend her without reservation."

—Denise Cline

Member at Law Offices of Denise Smith Cline, PLLC

"Betsy exemplifies the word *transformation* for that is what she offers all of her clients. Coaching with Betsy offers direct feedback and direct results!"

—Laura Gould

Owner/Coach at SwimLessonsRaleigh.com

"On a personal level, Betsy practices what she preaches. She never stops growing and learning."

—Will

"North Carolina's film industry was well served through Betsy's insight, hard work and commitment. Betsy championed projects that promoted the industry and was able to focus on the key issues that made a difference in how North Carolina competed against other states. She's a great ally to have on your team."

—Monty Hagler
President & CEO, RLF Communications

"Betsy Jordan is a visionary who can see beyond the routine tasks of the day. She has a gift for marketing and putting together resources to accomplish her goals. Betsy is a leader and can influence others with her keen insight, clear communication style and engaging personality."

—Bob Jamieson
Living Seaside Realty Group

"I was well served through Betsy's insight, hard work and commitment. She's a great ally to have on your team."

—Monty Hagler

"Betsy is a results oriented person, one you will be glad to have had the pleasure to meet, and delighted she's always working in your best interests."

—Carol Spiller, CMB

"Betsy Jordan has a keen insight into helping people achieve their life goals. She has an uncanny knack for breaking down barriers that may be creating obstacles for people that they cannot see for themselves: a frequent life-staller; spending time with Betsy is like drinking from a cold fountain on an incredibly hot day; you always want to come back for more! Take making a change in your life seriously and give Betsy a call; you won't be sorry!"

—Anna Watson Blair
Infusion Therapy Nurse at UNC-Hospitals

"Betsy is bright and highly intuitive. Her assistance with me at a critical point in my life's journey was instrumental in helping me in many areas, both professional and personal. Anyone hiring her will be rewarded many times over."

—Joe Christian

Performance Coach

"Betsy is an amazing business woman with dead-on intuition and a plethora of skills and experiences to draw from. I recommend her without reservation."

—Trish Thomas

CEO at Atomic20

"Betsy is a seasoned professional who brings her high energy level and professionalism to everything she does. Having her work with you and your company is a great investment."

—Teena Anderson

Non-Profit Organization Management Professional

KEY 3

MOVEMENT

WITH

COMPANION JOURNAL

Books By Betsy L. Jordan

Seven Absolute Keys to Create Anything:!

Coach! Seven Keys for the Beginning Coach

Key 1, Oneness, with Companion Journal

Key 2, Inter-Dimension, with Companion Journal

Key 3, Movement, with Companion Journal

Key 4, Paradox, with Companion Journal

Key 5, Exchange, with Companion Journal

Key 6, Personal Power, with Companion Journal

Key 7, Yin/Yang, with Companion Journal

BullsEye!

The Seven Tactics To Hit The Bull's Eye In Your Business

Film Industry Professional's Edition

Book One: Connect!

Book Two: See!

Book Three: Act!

Book Four: Experience!

Book Five: Expand!

Book Six: Power Up!

Book Seven: Launch!

KEY 3

MOVEMENT

WITH

COMPANION JOURNAL

BY BETSY L. JORDAN

Dedicated to my remarkable *mentors*.

They had their work cut out for them!

"The dance is a poem of which each movement is a word."

—Mata Hari

CONTENTS

AUTHOR'S NOTE

Many coaches will understand the principles covered herein automatically. My desire is that coaches use these universal principles of creativity and develop a language to use in their practices, troubleshooting as they go along. For example, the client who understands "oneness" and networks easily, may need work in the area of "personal power" if they are networking for approval. Or, a client who has no trouble imagining their future (inter-dimension) who yet won't get up off of the sofa needs work in the area of "movement." Let the seven keys be your framework.

Betsy Jordan

MOVEMENT, THE THIRD KEY

"If a writer knows enough about what he is writing about, he may omit things that he knows. The dignity of movement of an iceberg is due to only one ninth of it being above water."

—Ernest Hemingway

INTRODUCTION

The Difference

How many relationships, jobs, classes, experiences, great ideas, and coaching clients—even, have you experienced in your life? If we are alike in any way, you and I, it's probably safe to assume that we have both had great experiences and achievements, and have both had our share of failures and mishaps, too. In fact there is a lot that ten different jobs, three different careers, moving around the United States, one child, two stepsons, and two marriages will teach you, but the real difference came when I made a few simple changes in my life:

Focus and application.

As a positive, interested human being, I read, watched, listened, attended, and really did absorb a great deal of good information. Still, failure and success seemed somehow determined unconsciously and haphazardly until I focused on what were emerging as key principals and made very sure I applied what seemed true enough to possibly be universal. *Keys* started to rise to the top of my experiences when I employed attentive focus with application. Thrilling—simply thrilling. And today I get to share what I have learned with you, because my life after that point of discovery has been different, to say the least.

Seven *keys* unlock those doors you might have fought to get to, only to find them locked—the few keys that open to your own treasure trove of manifested dreams. These are the few really important doors in life, doors that lead to your own creativity and ability. What others call "luck" is explained in these pages.

But you've heard that before, right? In fact the bookstores are full of books making that very same claim, so what's the difference? Why read this book and others in my series? Simple. *You.* Let's be honest, there is a glut of information—good information—out there and probably even in your own library or on your own Kindle, so why read more? Well, the fact that you *are* reading more tells me two things: for all the good advice you've already found you want more which means you likely have *still* not completely found the right answers for *you*, and second, I believe most advisors do not allow into their equations the most important variable, which is, as I've said, *you*.

I want you to take the Seven Keys and make them yours, to understand these Seven Keys and apply them in *your own* way and to your unique situations and relationships. I want you to find these keys so natural after a period of focus and application that they become second nature, and what others see as a "knack" or "luck" seem to follow you wherever you go. I want you to have your own Midas touch as a result of your new acquaintance with *the Seven Keys*.

And there are seven. Some say this is the number of the mystic and indeed, throughout the ages seven has had a special place in the world. God created the heavens and the Earth in seven days. The Greek God Hermes is credited with scribing an ancient text with seven natural laws. Life itself is often described as having a seven-year cycle (or a seven-year itch). And after all of my own research and observation, the number seven simply seems to present itself universally, and in profound and powerful ways. So, seven it is.

And I now know there is *power* and an ability to *consciously create* what I really want, what you really want. Things are different now, thanks to that *knowledge*. And it did transition from a *belief* to a *knowledge* after consistently getting results with the seven keys. And when I consider sharing this knowledge it strikes me that I have plenty in my own life I wish I had *not* created, but to shy away from these things, you'll see, only pulls us back into the trap that beleaguers

5

most people, the belief that we *cannot* create our own thoughts, that we cannot manifest our own beauty and even our own greatness. In fact, even today when I end up with something that I am not consciously creating, I know that I get to learn from it, but I also know I get to move on from there to consciously change my own thoughts in order to create something different, something desirable. I know that there is power and the ability to consciously create what I really want, when I am fully accountable for it all.

You choose: which is more empowering, when you blame circumstances or people around you for anything non-ideal in your life *or* knowing that you are responsible for all of your life *and can therefore change it?* Important choice to make. And your life is happening *now and you are in it*—this is not a "waiting room" by any means. Too many valuable people still see it that way.

In fact the former choice is actually the more practical one, and before you take any knowledge and consider it, it should, after all, be practical. All my roads have led me here. I have studied with various people, as mentioned I've read, listened, watched, attended, and I've experimented with my own life. I have things in my own background you would be very able to relate to: failures and successes. There are enough of the first that would make us empathetic friends, and plenty of the second that would establish my credibility to lead on this issue, to capture your imagination for self- and world-improvement, just as the discovery of these seven keys has captured mine.

Anyone can learn these seven keys, either for oneself or as a philosophy with which to help others. We all create our worlds subconsciously everyday anyway, why not take charge of that facility? This book is an attempt to give you the tools that I now apply in my own life and my own practice, and these tools can now be shortcuts for you and your own clients!

But it's not magic, either. Learning to be aware takes practice.

Although some very important parts of the process cannot be "seen," they are as real as those parts that you can see. In fact, the world of the "unseen" is arguably more important than the world of the "seen," and this will become more clear as we move forward. With each key that we explain you (and your clients) will be given a chance to work with it, to do exercises which give you a practical experience of the key. I have found—through my own experience and through information that frankly, has simply come through me—that each key has a corresponding chakra, or area in the energetic body to which it corresponds. The chakra system is an energetic system which is explained through Vedic science, and which the Hindu religion has located just outside of the body but close to very specific areas of connection. You can use these areas of the body as touch points to remember the Seven Keys. Other than that, please see the appendix on the chakras at the back of this book and visit texts on the chakra system to understand more about that connection. My intention here is to keep things simple.

The way that I believe creativity comes through most quickly is from the 7th chakra down. In other words, I believe creativity can best be explained from the spiritual plane through manifestation, from the intellectual to the material, and from head to toe. You have a thought, the thought becomes manifest after action is taken.

Yet you do not have to believe this to benefit from the exercises or the information. My intention is to give you the tools to build a foundation for creating the life you dream of, with confidence that you are in tune with the natural elements of the universe, and to do so as quickly as possible.

I wish you all you have ever dreamed of.

And once you've assembled your own *Seven Keys* with focus and application, how will your life be different? How will your coaching practice change? And who will you help?

"It takes a lot of courage to release the familiar and seemingly secure, to embrace the new. But there is no real security in what is no longer meaningful. There is more security in the adventurous and exciting, for in movement there is life, and in change there is power."

—Alan Cohen

GET'M MOVING!

Have you ever wanted to fire a client.? Many times I have been in conversations with a client and felt like they were standing somewhere in the parking lot, not anywhere near the court that they were playing on. I know the use of athletic metaphors in coaching isn't useful for some, but most of my clients understand that I'm not going to coach them if they're standing in the parking lot. I'm not gonna go out to the parking to get them. I'm not going to do anything but say, "Come back to me when you're ready to play ball."

It's imperative that—along with this wonderful, beautiful action plan you've designed with your clients, and this wonderful vision you can get them into, and this enthusiastic way of approaching life that you can inspire them into—it's very important that you hold out, that you have them take action. That you let them know that a good story and guilt is not the same thing as taking action.

All this talk about the "secret" and visualizing and getting themselves into the experience of having their dreams happen is for naught, if they do not take action on their vision.

If they don't *move*.

Sometimes that action makes them feel really uncomfortable. It's easier to sit back and dream, and dream, and dream. Remind them that great things begin with a single step. Remind them in the words of Yoda "Do or do not. There is no try." (Yet there is not just the doing, there's the being. And we know that.)

So by taking action and moving one step after another step after another step great things do happen and will happen for them. So the Key of Movement is not just moving, even though it is a universal principle of creativity. The answer is rather "directed movement," movement that is conscious and voluntary. And *vision* is the special sauce.

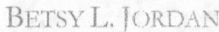

"Many a trip continues long after movement in time and space have ceased."

—John Steinbeck

ACTION!

J ust do it! . . . Just do it? Easier said than done? Maybe not, maybe it is that easy. Maybe a painter really just has to swat his brush on a clean canvas *that first time* to get the art flowing again. Some writers and artists say that's the secret to creative and writing blocks. And when we don't "swat" we can spiral out of our known universe, dwelling in a cesspool of self doubt and fear, considering how irrelevant we really "are."

Imagine all the great potential that is literally wasted, which dies on the vine and never even has a chance thanks to inactivity, to non-starts.

Is there a way to change this? Because we all seem to suffer to inaction to some degree.

Yes, and it's kind of magical. It's *movement*. 'Just do it" *is* an effective message and lots of people like and relate to it, obviously, but it would be better, more appropriate to use the term more closely related to the key found in nature of *movement*. "Just start moving" might be a better slogan—at least a more useful one.

Movement of course, is literally a start of motion, and things can happen. Stasis is the problem—nothing moving but internal thought. When you do start moving the magic that takes place looks like this: You decide on an action. You take action.. You encounter *resistance* in and of the physical universe, whether it's opposition, other ideas, or simply the wind pushing back now that you are moving. But what happens when you encounter the trappings of movement is you, as a creative being, begin creating alternatives along the way.

Life is a contact sport (I know, more sports metaphors!). Feel it! Isn't that why we play sports in the first place? That and actually scoring goals, winning games, learning from defeat.

What's so exciting and oft overlooked is that *new ideas* emerge when we are in action. An entrepreneur I know failed to launch any of his great ideas one year, and so decided to launch one a month the following year. The exercise was revealing. With each idea he sought to launch he found new ideas sprouted, and from them new ideas sprouted, and...

Motion can be magic.

Perfection is the enemy of *getting going*. *Nothing* can be perfect, even as some things do get or seem close. But there is "perfect enough." Concern about perfection can often be a paralyzing factor.

How many clients stay in a job they hate and don't get moving out of fear and "logic?" You can get moving even if it's on a small scale. And even that small motion can trigger different kinds of magic. Creativity and experience can take place. Without movement they cannot.

"Music is the movement of sound to reach the soul for the education of its virtue."

—Plato

CAVES ARE FOR BEARS

Many Moms will say this as they put yet another box in the attic: "I must put this equipment, or these project supplies away just in case," or "I can't part with [fill in the blank], it feels like I'm betraying my dead aunt, uncle, mom, dad," or "That was a gift from my third ex-wife and reminds me of a happy time," and so on.

Stuff that we hold on to can soon define who we are. It's as if we choose certain items which anchor us to our pasts—we're afraid that by moving forward, we'll drift in the sea of life. Sometimes, our stuff anchors us so strongly to our past, that we don't feel a pull to our future. Our future feels risky while our past feels comforting, comfortable.

Havens are meant to be places you return to once you've been out in the world. And caves are for hibernating bears, not for humans to disappear into.

Sure, taking risks can be frightening. In fact, generally, that's the nature of risk-taking. Yet, you grow stagnant, backward and rutty when nothing is hazarded. There's no conflict to spur growth, no chop to the sea, and you waste away.

What are you using to anchor yourself to your past? What can you release today?

"One individual can begin a movement that turns the tide of history. Martin Luther King in the civil rights movement, Mohandas Gandhi in India, Nelson Mandela in South Africa are examples of people standing up with courage and non-violence to bring about needed changes."

—Jack Canfield

FORWARD

With one single step, John Glenn stood on the moon. Maxims like, "Take baby steps," and "One step at a time"—we've heard them all. And it's true, if we're moving forward, we're not moving backward.

Have you ever driven a car solely looking in the rear-view mirror? Dee Messina sings of leaving her former lover:

> *Bye Bye Love, I'll catch ya later.*
> *Gotta lead foot down on my accelerator,*
> *and the rear view mirror torn off*
> *'cause I ain't never looking back.*

We advocate keeping your rear-view in case you need to travel back-end first. That's the only time we want you to go looking backwards.

Moving forward takes you in the direction of your bull's-eye. It's that with where you're aiming when you're looking backward, you'll never get there.

"A society should never become like a pond with stagnant water, without movement. That's the most important thing."

—Mikhail Gorbachev

LIKE WATER

Think about what happens when you say "I'm going to quit some habit," whether it's smoking or over-eating or driving too fast. When you say it and speak it, before you do that, you consider who you're saying it to, don't you? If you say it to one person they're going to hold your feet to the fire. If you say it to another person, they may not care. But either way you've declared it, so you've made a promise, even if it's only to yourself.

The Key of Movement begins with the most subtle of life's movements which is *speech*. In the beginning there was the word. When you speak something you bring it into being, you take an action. If you just sit there, and say nothing, we human beings don't really know what's going on. So once you speak it, you create a movement. There's movement all around us, everywhere, constantly. There are cells moving in our bodies, we're thankful that our hearts are beating.

There's a principle of movement that you can have working with you or you can work against it. So if you speak where it comes from a motivation to hurt or to take something from someone or to criticize someone., you're creating something that can be a very negative thing. If we are conscious of what we speak, speaking is a powerful thing.

So I focused on speaking in terms of how I express the concept of movement, or the Key of Movement. But of course there are a lot of other ways we can talk about that. In creating a product, for example, there can be things called bottlenecks, where movement is restricted. What you want is for things to be flowing, for things to regenerate and flow through Even in your product processes, you want them to be moving and moving and moving—you don't want inventory to sit there too long.

Same thing is true of your thoughts. You want them to progress in a natural evolution. And then you want to speak them or to talk it out. If you find yourself being closed off emotionally, you need to find someone to talk to or scream it out at a pillow or do something—dance, move, move to a different part of the room, whatever. And your *thoughts* will change.

Use this principle in your creativity. Use it. Work with the *movement*. Be conscious and aware of it, that things constantly change. If you resist that change, you're resisting a principle of the universe and it will show up somewhere else. Movement is like water, it will move around if it can't go through. So you are always creating motion in some direction.

Let it be the one that you want and desire.

"Walking is magic. Can't recommend it highly enough. I read that Plato and Aristotle did much of their brilliant thinking together while ambulating. The movement, the meditation, the health of the blood pumping, and the rhythm of footsteps... this is a primal way to connect with one's deeper self."

—Paula Cole

CONCLUSION

The Seven Keys are here for you, unearthed and available to you. I can show and describe them but only you can pick them up and approach your goals and dreams with them, ready to unlock the barriers so many others find impassable. It's my hope that you *try* them after understanding them, that you perfect their use, that you use this and all books on the subject to improve first your own life and then the lives of your clients. I hope they become second nature to you. All of us can benefit massively from a knowledge of the Seven Keys and if we coach others they become even more important, so that we and our clients can create what we want, right where we are. We no longer need to wonder, be frustrated, or seek the approval of others or even the environment.

Armed with this book series you can make a difference. These books are not the fastest route, however, to learning the Seven Keys and their application. That comes from a live event, where through your own commitment and focus, your results will be fast and powerful. See the back of this book to discover how you can attend a seminar or webinar, how you can become certified in the training of others in The Seven Keys, and how you too can benefit from receiving coaching as well as from delivering it. It might be easier than you think to get connected, but even were it not, what would it be worth to train in tapping into your own massive creativity? What about your clients?

And never think that seeking improvement suggests you lack in any way. You have all you need right now, right where you are. The trick is getting to it. We are each whole and complete beings, with untapped potential and an opportunity for actualization. We can each make our dreams come true. Holding a client, friend, or loved one to a higher standard is also not to make less of someone, but more, especially if they themselves desire it. Many don't seem to desire it simply because they are unaware or do not believe it's possible. We know better.

You are uniquely you, and the only one. And you are complete. You only need to unlock what lies inside.

I hope that you take these keys and unlocking your barriers, live the life I believe you deserve. I hope you find abundance in all you seek in whatever arenas you find you love, and in whatever form this may be. I hope you find this all to be an incredible adventure, because it is just that—the adventure of *you*. And you have gifts for the world, that the world needs and needs badly.

Give a man a fish and he eats for perhaps a day, but teach him to fish and he can feed himself, his family, his friends and community as long as there are fish. And when we create abundance for those around us we seem to have it ourselves. When we see strength, intelligence, goodness in others and grant them as much we have effectively created those things or at least planted the seeds of those things. The opposite is, well, the opposite. *Pity,* for example. When given or received leads to weakness and a weakened relationship as well. Any immediate gratification is short lived, of course. In fact taken to an extreme, this is the road to resentment! Giving when you lack leads only to more lack if you are giving only with the intention of feeling better or bigger yourself. Giving from a place of abundance however, creates it for everyone.

Giving with the idea of improving someone else's life *while also* improving your own is about one of life's greatest answers. The greatest partnerships—whether it's a husband and wife, business partners, or even a coach and client—are created by two wholly independent people who choose to be together because they can and want to be together. Partnerships created out of dependency leave one partner stronger than the other. They spiral downward as they are based on contraction, lack, and fear.

Yet we are, each of us, whole and complete beings.

And there is nothing broken about you or your clients, only untapped, locked away, in ways unique to each client. In fact we only do maintenance and development here, the repair shop is somewhere else. And part of that development is first recognizing, which is easy to do, the magnificence in each person. All you need to do is look.

May you celebrate your magnificence and that of each client through a life of passionate work and sound knowledge, may you and those you help then bring your own special gifts to the world!

Grounded in the Key of Oneness,

Understanding the influence of the Key of Inter-Dimension,

And executing the Key of Movement,

You create what you want with zero boundaries.

"To me, if life boils down to one thing, it's movement. To live is to keep moving."

—Jerry Seinfeld

The 7 Keys

To Creating The Life You Have Dreamed Of!

Key #1, Oneness

Key #2, Inter-Dimension

Key #3, Movement

Key #4, Paradox

Key #5, Exchange

Key #6, Personal Power

Key #7, Yin~Yang

COMPANION JOURNAL

"Though we may never be able to comprehend human life, we know certainly that it is a movement, of whatever nature it be. The existence of movement unavoidably implies a body which is being moved and a force which is moving it. Hence, wherever there is life, there is a mass moved by a force. All mass possesses inertia; all force tends to persist."

—Nikola Tesla

Exercise ~ Do or Do Not

For the exercise of movement it's important to be very literal.

1. Take a pencil or pen, it doesn't matter which. Drop it on the ground.

2. Try to pick up the pen or the pencil. The task is not to actually pick up the pencil—it's to *try* to pick up the pencil.

3. Try again.

4. And try again.

5. Turn around.

6. Try to pick up the pencil backwards.

7. Now pick up the pencil or pen.

8. Notice the difficulty in "trying" to do something relative to just doing it.

9. Now just do it.

Exercise ~ Choose Your Words

This one is simple. An exercise for the Key of Movement is to watch what happens when you use words of love. Also watch what happens when you choose words of anger. Watch what happens as you breathe.

The key of vibration is incredible and critical.

Exercise ~ Unlocking with The Keys

The key of oneness explains the idea that if we are arguing with someone in this part of the world, this leaves a mark on someone else in another place. It's not a chain reaction or anything as clearly direct, yet it has an effect just the same. It explains why Mother Teresa would say, "You will not see me at an anti-war rally. If you have a peace rally, please invite me." She understood oneness, as well as polarity or paradox and expansion versus contraction. She knew we are all connected, she knew to focus on the thing that is the highest and best good to get the results she wanted, and she also knew that what she placed her attention on would expand.

All of the keys overlap. The process of creativity is integrated and happens regardless of what we think about it. We are always breathing, our blood is always pumping. We create new cells in our body every second. With every thought that we think; we are creating. At the level of thought and emotion, we can affect things in the world that we do not see.

In the following exercise, when we tested it, we found that it was effective in demonstrating that we can affect others simply by our thoughts and feelings. I was surprised when we discovered that the person with their eyes closed would often respond or react and not even be aware of their reactions! I see this exercise now as a way to illustrate the key of exchange, the key of oneness, the key of inter-dimension, the key of paradox, the key of personal power on a subtle level. However, I believe it applies best to the key of movement as it clearly shows we affect others by our own thoughts, and that once we accept that we do, we can affect everything around us by never even saying a word.

1. Put one person in the front of the room with their eyes closed or blindfolded.

2. You or someone else act as facilitator, and you whisper to other participants a word such as joy, sexiness, frustration, etc.

3. The participants go up one by one and without saying a word, they do their best to generate the word that they are given in the person who has their eyes closed.

4. After a short while ask the person at the front of the
    room to open his or her eyes or remove the blindfold,
    and talk about their thoughts during the exercise.

"I don't harp on the negative because if you do, then there's no progression. There's no forward movement. You got to always look on the bright side of things, and we are in control. Like, you have control over the choices you make."

—Taraji P. Henson

ABOUT BETSY JORDAN

Betsy Jordan holds a PhD in Experiential Training through the Legacy Center, and Direct Impact. Further training in leadership development and coaching helped her focus on how we can effectively cause transformation in our lives and businesses. "The river that runs through my career is the exciting world of human development." She has studied with Deepak Chopra, MD., becoming one of the first mind/body educators in the country. "Studying with Deepak helped me to see the science behind thoughts causing reactions in our bodies". That degree opened doors for her work in quality customer service with major corporations in hospital supplies and banking industries. Betsy has a BS in Business Administration from the University of North Carolina at Chapel Hill.

Betsy's life experiences have encompasses the creative community, the corporate world and the unique challenges of entrepreneurship. Whatever challenges you face, she is the coach who can relate, resolve problems, and turbo-charge your results. Her pioneering work on creativity is published in her book, *Seven Absolute Keys to Create Anything!* as well as a number of forthcoming publications. Please watch for new titles and materials as they are released.

START TODAY!

THE TIME TO BEGIN your perfecting of the seven keys is *right now*. Your full life of passion, your independence from waiting on politicians to gain their senses or the film industry to seek you out is at hand.

www.BullsEyeCoach.com

SEMINARS & WEBINARS

FIND OUT ABOUT UPCOMING seminars and webinars by visiting this website:

www.BullsEyeCoach.com

COACHING

AND FOR YOUR QUICKEST route to perfecting the seven tactics and to experience The BullsEyeCoaching™ process (which includes the seven tactics), *contact me today*. I look forward to meeting you and hearing your ideas!

info@BullsEyeCoach.com

ACKNOWLEDGEMENTS

THIS IS A WORK about life. I could say that I thank everyone who ever touched my life directly and indirectly for all of you have been teachers, and I mean that sincerely. In this way, you all have contributed to the writing of this book.

To my mentors, all of you: Ray, Michael, Lori, Rob, James, Sam. Let me leave a special notice to my mentor, Deepak Chopra, whose groundbreaking work in the psycho-physiological origins of disease taught me so much about how the mind and the body are related. Through Carolyn Myss in her *Anatomy of the Spirit* I recognize that even in irreverence there is still reverence.

Thanks to Louise Hay whose bravery and generosity has helped so many people overcome ailments in the body. To my mentors at the legacy center, Robb and Lori in particular, I thank you so much for the true stand you are in the world for so many people. For my mentor Michael Strasner who sees the humor in all things and always finds that balance.

To my former husbands both of whom taught me the extraordinary strength and power of faith. To the great loves of my life who are numerous and so I would rather they know who they are and be grateful that we had that love. Once I choose to love someone, I *always* do, even if we disagree.

Sean Roach, I wouldn't have ever thought about writing these books if not for your brilliance and direction. And Rodney Miles, thank you so much for your contribution above expectations and execution of this series. I look forward to many, many years with this team of amazing people.

To the boys of my heart, Kyle and Taylor, who taught me that parenting had nothing to do with being of the same genetic make-up. And finally, to my sensitive and brilliant daughter who shows me every day what a miracle life is.

THE CHAKRAS

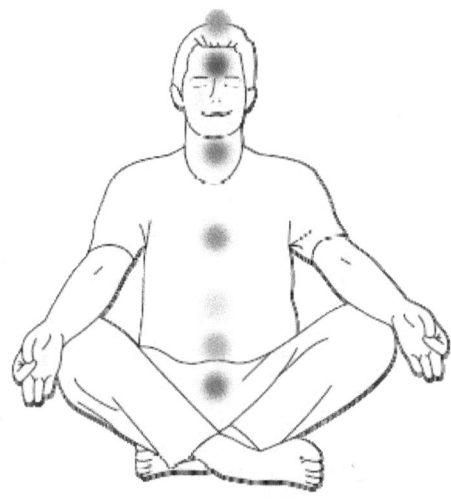

Figure 1: The seven chakras and their locations in the body.

The word "chakra" comes from a Sanskrit word meaning "wheel," (or "spinning point of light) and in some religions of India are considered points of energy and part of the intangible body that influences the physical body. Energy channels through these points. While there are believed to be many and various *nodes* or chakras throughout our bodies, these are the seven most important.

According to Caroline Myss in her book *Anatomy of the Spirit,* all of our thoughts and experiences are filtered through these chakras which function in part as databases, and are associated with our physical and mental selves as well as certain colors.

Some associate the chakras with specific nerve centers and glandular functions, and each is associated with various energies, all of which can be understood and placed into harmony.

THE 7 KEYS

TO CREATING THE LIFE YOU HAVE DREAMED OF!

Key #1, Oneness

Key #2, Inter-Dimension

Key #3, Movement

Key #4, Paradox

Key #5, Exchange

Key #6, Personal Power

Key #7, Yin~Yang

7 KEYS SUMMARIES

Key 1, Oneness

Oneness, all, we are the same stuff, we affect and are affected by each other, remove judgment of self and others.

Located above the head. 7th Chakra.

Key 2, Inter-Dimension

Inter-dimension, all levels, all of the time, awareness at the level of "before language," thoughts become things, know what you "know."

Located between the eyes (third eye). 6th Chakra.

Key 3, Movement

Movement, constant motion even at subtle levels… everything moving, language is the great creator, in the beginning was the Word, Thumper in the movie *Bambi* was correct: "If you can't say somethin' nice, don't say nothin' at all." Even subtler, if you can't "think "anything nice, then don't think anything at all, or at the very least, get outta the room!

Located at the throat (voice box). 5th Chakra.

Key 4, Paradox

Paradox, in every challenge lies the seed of its solution. Opposites exist. Polarity. Focus on positive and dismiss all lack and thoughts of lack. Want lots of goodies in your life, warm and fuzzies? Create it for others. Want love? Create it in every interaction. What we focus on expands. Decide with the heart.

Located above the heart. 4th Chakra.

Key 5, Exchange

Exchange, the Universe (God) rewards expansive plans. Giving and receiving both are expansive actions. Taking is a contracting energy—it interrupts expansion and leads to contraction. Give what you most want in a manner that creates this for others. Associated with gut feeling or solar plexus.

Located above the solar plexus. 3rd Chakra.

Key 6, Personal Power

Personal power, we are all whole and complete, no matter what our size and shape, number of fingers and toes, we can never give our power away. In our most complete and powerful understanding of ourselves, we understand the laws of cause and effect. We are able to respond to it all. Owning our power means that we have released "victim" consciousness. From the place of personal strength, ownership of it all, we can create something different. There is nothing more powerful than *you!*

Located above the abdomen. 2nd Chakra.

Key 7, Yin/Yang

Male/female, there lies within us the feminine and masculine principles and properties of creativity. Feminine is nurturing, gestational, conceptual, and spiritual. Masculine is assertive, action-oriented, physical, and material. When in balance, beautiful and powerful creations are born. When out of balance, depression and sometimes even war ensue.

Located at the root or genital area. 1st Chakra.

7 KEYS & THE CHAKRAS

Key #1, Oneness
Located above the head. 7th Chakra.

Key #2, Inter-Dimension
Located between the eyes (third eye). 6th Chakra.

Key #3, Movement
Located at the throat (voice box). 5th Chakra.

Key #4, Paradox
Located above the heart. 4th Chakra.

Key #5, Exchange
Located above the solar plexus. 3rd Chakra.

Key #6, Personal Power
Located above the abdomen. 2nd Chakra.

Key #7, Yin~Yang
Located at the root or genital area. 1st Chakra.

SUCCESS STORIES

The following case studies assure you that the process works! And this format keeps us from sharing confidential information.

THE LESSON

Do it Your Way

A frustrated employee turned budding entrepreneur discovered her true path.

This client came to me knowing that things weren't right at work. She'd known this for awhile. She wanted guidance. In pattern interruption the image she pulled was of her on the beach talking with Jesus. (This image is always the perfect one for you, chosen by you, in the perfect time to answer your intended result.) His words, according to what she saw were, "You go back and do what you need to do. I am with you. I've done this my way, you do it your way." I watched her progress from afar. After this experience, she had the courage to start her business. It is gradually growing—her way. It's a great gift to the world, and a great gift from her heart. The image she held in her mind's eye that day gave her strength, courage and insight to boldly proceed in the direction of her dreams.

THE LESSON
The Power of Saying, "No"

A very powerful educated attorney had a vision, yet didn't know what to do about it.

My trademarked seven-step TurboCoaching program showed us that the step involving personal power was out of balance. Once this client got clear on his vision for his company, he was able to make requests with urgency. This got him an audience with a major U.S. corporate CEO which led to a future relationship with that corporate leader. Two months was all he needed. His life and his work were transformed, and his vision came to life.

THE LESSON
Don't Ignore the Shadow Side

Yet another study involved a public relations professional.

Her life was grounded in involvement with people. She knew her professional life was in good shape; yet her personal relationships would falter. She chose pattern interruption and discovered a subconscious stumbling block. The image in her subconscious was of her dad. During the session she pulled an image showing that she adored him, and then, she saw a dark side that she had never consciously acknowledged. Through the interpretation session she was able to see that she denied the shadow side in any of her relationships. Once she was aware of this pattern of denial, she was able to create relationships with people which were authentic, embracing both the lighter and darker sides of their personalities. When those sides were extreme, she could walk away without harm.

www.ingramcontent.com/pod-product-compliance
Lightning Source LLC
Chambersburg PA
CBHW060349190526
45169CB00002B/539